But Smoking Makes Me Happy

THE LINK BETWEEN NICOTINE AND DEPRESSION

Tobacco: The Deadly Drug

But Smoking Makes Me Happy

THE LINK BETWEEN NICOTINE AND DEPRESSION

by
David Hunter

But Smoking Makes Me Happy: The Link Between
Nicotine and Depression

MASON CREST PUBLISHERS INC.
370 Reed Road
Broomall, Pennsylvania 19008
(866)MCP-BOOK (toll free)
www.masoncrest.com

First Printing

9 8 7 6 5 4 3 2 1

ISBN 978-1-4222-0244-9
ISBN 978-1-4222-0230-2 (series)
          Library of Congress Cataloging-in-Publication Data
Hunter, David.
  But smoking makes me happy : the link between nicotine and
depression / David Hunter.
      p. cm. — (Tobacco : the deadly drug)
  Includes bibliographical references and index.
  ISBN 978-1-4222-0244-9   ISBN 978-1-4222-1335-3
  1. Smoking—Juvenile literature. 2. Tobacco use—Physiological
effect—Juvenile literature. 3. Depression, Mental—Juvenile
literature. I. Title.
  RC567.H864 2009
  616.86'50651—dc22
                              2008023306

Design by MK Bassett-Harvey.
Produced by Harding House Publishing Service, Inc.
www.hardinghousepages.com
Cover design by Peter Culotta.
Printed in The United States of America.

Contents

Introduction

Tobacco has been around for centuries. In fact, it played a major role in the early history of the United States. Tobacco use has fallen into and out of popularity, sometimes based on gender roles or class, or more recently, because of its effects on health. The books in the Mason Crest series TOBACCO: THE DEADLY DRUG, provide readers with a look at many aspects of tobacco use. Most important, the series takes a serious look at why smoking is such a hard habit to break, even with all of the available information about its harmful effects.

The primary ingredient in tobacco products that keeps people coming back for another cigarette is nicotine. Nicotine is a naturally occurring chemical in the tobacco plant. As plants evolved over millions of years, they developed the ability to produce chemical defenses against being eaten by animals. Nicotine is the tobacco plant's chemical defense weapon. Just as too much nicotine can make a person feel dizzy and nauseated, so the same thing happens to animals that might otherwise eat unlimited quantities of the tobacco plant.

Nicotine, in small doses, produces mildly pleasurable (rewarding) experiences, leading many people to dose themselves repeatedly throughout the day. People carefully dose themselves with nicotine to maximize the rewarding experience. These periodic hits of tobacco also help people avoid unpleasant (toxic) effects, such as dizziness, nausea, trembling, and sweating, which can occur when someone takes in an excessive amount of nicotine. These unpleasant effects are sometimes seen when a person smokes for the first time.

Although nicotine is the rewarding component of cigarettes, it is not the cause of many diseases that trouble smokers, such as lung cancer, heart attacks, and strokes. Many of the thousands of other chemicals in the cigarette are responsible for the increased risk for these diseases among smokers. In some cases, medical research has identified cancer-causing chemicals in the burning cigarette. More research is needed, because our understanding of exactly how cigarette smoking causes many forms of cancer, lung diseases (emphysema, bronchitis), heart attacks, and strokes is limited, as is our knowledge on the effects of secondhand smoke.

The problem with smoking also involves addiction. But what is addiction? Addiction refers to a pattern of behavior, lasting months to years, in which a person engages in the intense, daily use of a pleasure-producing (rewarding) activity, such as smoking. This type of use has medically and personally negative effects for the person. As an example of negative medical consequences, consider that heavy smoking (nicotine addiction) leads to heart attacks and lung cancer. As an example of negative personal consequences, consider that heavy smoking may cause a loss of friendship, because the friend can't tolerate the smoke and/or the odor.

Nicotine addiction includes tolerance and withdrawal. New smokers typically start with fewer than five cigarettes per day. Gradually, as the body becomes adapted to the presence of nicotine, greater amounts are required to obtain the same rewarding effects, and the person eventually smokes fifteen to twenty or more cigarettes per day. This is tolerance, meaning that more drug is needed to achieve the same rewarding effects. The brain becomes "wired" differently after long-term exposure to nicotine, allowing the brain to tolerate levels of nicotine that would otherwise be toxic and cause nausea, vomiting, dizziness and anxiety.

When a heavy smoker abruptly stops smoking, irritability, headache, sleeplessness, anxiety, and difficulty concentrating all develop within half a day and trouble the smoker for one to two weeks. These withdrawal effects are generally the opposite of those produced by the drug. They are another external sign that the brain has become wired differently because of long-term exposure to nicotine. The withdrawal effects described above are accompanied by craving. For the nicotine addict, craving is a state of mind in which having a cigarette seems the most important thing in life at the moment. For the nicotine addict, craving is a powerful urge to smoke.

Nicotine addiction, then, can be understood as heavy, daily use over months to years (with tolerance and withdrawal), despite negative consequences. Now that we have definitions of *nicotine* and *addiction*, why read the books in this series? The answer is simple: tobacco is available everywhere to persons of all ages. The books in the series TOBACCO: THE DEADLY DRUG are about understanding the beginnings, natural history, and consequences of nicotine addiction. If a teenager smokes at least one cigarette daily for a month, that person has an 80 percent chance of becoming a lifetime, nicotine-addicted, daily smoker, with all the negative consequences.

But the series is not limited to those topics. What are the characteristic beginnings of nicotine addiction? Nicotine addiction typically begins between the ages of twelve and twenty, when most young people decide to try a first cigarette. Because cigarettes are available everywhere in our society, with little restriction on purchase, nearly everyone is faced with the decision to take a puff from that first cigarette. Whether this first puff leads to a lifetime of nicotine addiction depends on several factors. Perhaps the most important factor is DNA (genetics), as twin studies tell us that most of the risk for nicotine addiction is genetic, but there is a large role for nongenetic factors (environment), such as the smoking habits of friends. Research is needed to identify the specific genetic and environmental factors that shape a person's decision to continue to smoke after that first cigarette. Books in the series also address how peer pressure and biology affect one's likelihood of smoking and possibly becoming addicted.

It is difficult to underestimate the power of nicotine addiction. It causes smokers to continue to smoke despite life-threatening events. When heavy smokers have a heart attack, a life-threatening event often directly related to smoking, they spend a week or more in the hospital where they cannot smoke. So they are discharged after enforced abstinence. Even though they realize that smoking contributed strongly to the heart attack, half of them return to their former smoking habits within three weeks of leaving the hospital. This decision to return to smoking increases the risk of a second heart attack. Nicotine addiction can influence powerfully the choices we make, often prompting us to make choices that put us at risk.

TOBACCO: THE DEADLY DRUG doesn't stop with the whys and the hows of smoking and addiction. The series includes books that provide readers with tools they can use to not take that first cigarette, how they can stand up to negative peer pressure, and know when they are being unfairly influenced by the media. And if they do become smokers, books in the series provide information about how they can stop.

If nicotine addiction can be a powerful negative effect, then giving people information that might help them decide to avoid—or stop—smoking makes sense. That is what TOBACCO: THE DEADLY DRUG is all about.

— *Wade Berrettini MD, PhD*

CHAPTER

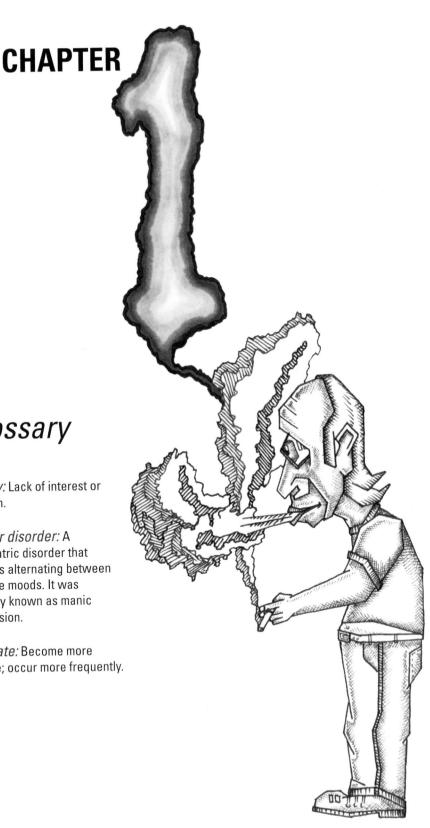

Glossary

apathy: Lack of interest or emotion.

bipolar disorder: A psychiatric disorder that involves alternating between extreme moods. It was formerly known as manic depression.

escalate: Become more intense; occur more frequently.

A Look at Nicotine and Depression

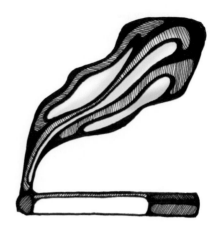

Today, some scientists believe there may be some connection between nicotine—an addictive chemical substance found in tobacco that acts a stimulant—and depression. Studies have observed a relationship between those suffering from depression and those who smoke cigarettes, one of the primary means of taking in nicotine.

Many people suffering from depression are addicted to nicotine. For example, some patients in the psychiatric unit at Johns Hopkins Hospital in Baltimore, Maryland, are dependent on cigarettes. This unit most frequently treats people with depression and *bipolar disorder*. While in the unit, patients must keep to a strict schedule. They wake up at 7:00 a.m. and eat breakfast from 8:00 to 8:30. Most patients attend the morn-

Many people rely on nicotine for their happiness; without it they become irritable and depressed.

ing community meeting at 9:00. Built into this schedule are regular breaks for the patients to go outside into a courtyard to smoke cigarettes. The smokers always out-number the nonsmokers on the unit by a great margin. Any alteration of this schedule can disturb the patients who are smokers. For one woman in particular, the smoke break seems like an essential part of her day. Much of the time, this woman's difficult behavior is a trial for the nurses who care for her. She is often rude and uncoop-erative, mumbling insults at the nurses when she sees them, refusing to take her medication, and even refus-ing to bathe.

When this patient begins to behave this way, the nurses tell her she can't have her smoke break. Almost instantly, her attitude improves. She apologizes to every-one around her, and she cooperates with the nurses' suggestions and requests. The possibility of missing her smoke break is an extremely powerful motivator.

In reality, the nurses on the unit almost never deny any of their patients a smoke break. Doing so would invite open hostility from the patients. Their psychiatric symptoms, especially their depression, would *escalate*.

The situation at John Hopkins is just one illustration of the perceived connection between depression and nicotine. Clearly, many of these patients rely heavily on their cigarette-smoking habit. Before delving into the relationship between the medi-cal condition of depression and nicotine addiction, it is important to understand each part of the equation.

What Is Depression?

Depression is a serious and common medical condition. Intense and persistent sadness is one of the most common symptoms in people with clinical depression. People suffering from depression may also have a lack of energy, loss of interest in their favorite activities, an inability to concentrate or think clearly, and changes in their normal sleep routines. Feelings of anger, loneliness, hopelessness, and *apathy* are common as well. Some may even experience physical pain connected to their condition.

A widespread disease, depression is experienced by roughly 14.8 million adults in the United States in any given year. This translates to about 5 percent of the country's population. Women seem to be especially vulnerable, experiencing the disease at about twice the rate of men, according to a 2005 report from the National Institute of Mental Health. Despite the prevalence of the illness, depression often goes undiagnosed by doctors, and many people who have depression never seek any type of medical attention for their condition.

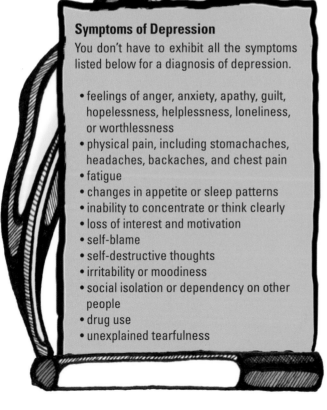

Symptoms of Depression

You don't have to exhibit all the symptoms listed below for a diagnosis of depression.

- feelings of anger, anxiety, apathy, guilt, hopelessness, helplessness, loneliness, or worthlessness
- physical pain, including stomachaches, headaches, backaches, and chest pain
- fatigue
- changes in appetite or sleep patterns
- inability to concentrate or think clearly
- loss of interest and motivation
- self-blame
- self-destructive thoughts
- irritability or moodiness
- social isolation or dependency on other people
- drug use
- unexplained tearfulness

To an outside observer, a person with depression may simply seem upset or "blue." Some may view this behavior as a response to difficult times or stressful circumstances. Depression, however, is more complicated than a result of suffering some type of personal   loss or crisis. These situations can make a person's depression worse, but they are not its sole cause.

Depression is a serious illness that requires medical intervention. Sometimes well-meaning people tell those suffering from depression that their condition is "all in their heads," but it is not. A person who is depressed may feel hopeless. This feeling of despondency may lead to thoughts of suicide. Although most people with depression never attempt suicide, individuals are more likely to attempt to take their own lives if

Although most depressed people never attempt to commit suicide, depression does make people more likely to take their own lives.

they are depressed than if they are not. Each year, suicide claims more than 30,000 lives in the United States. Around the world, about 3,000 people take their own lives each day, according to the World Health Organization. Depression is one of the primary factors leading to suicide. At least two-thirds of people who attempt suicide are depressed at the time they try to take their lives.

Depression can have a negative impact on a person's health, even if he or she has no thoughts of suicide. People with major depression are over 2.3 times more likely to die from certain conditions, such as heart disease, than are people who do not have depression. Other studies have shown that people with depression may be more likely to develop Type 2 diabetes. Overall, depression worsens other medical conditions—such as diabetes or heart disease—and decreases people's chances of regaining their health.

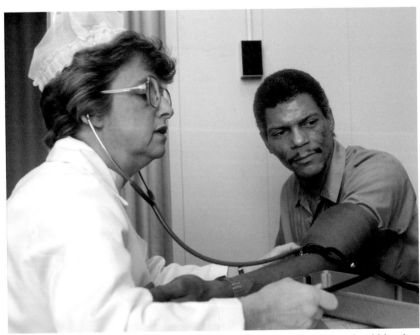

Nicotine can affect the whole body; these effects may include raised blood pressure.

Nicotine and Depression

Nicotine affects the whole body, increasing a person's heart rate and blood pressure. It also can change a person's mood by signaling the brain to release more of a chemical known as dopamine. Dopamine is a chemical messenger—called a neurotransmitter—involved in the pleasure system of the brain. Most researchers believe that neurotransmitters play a major role in depression. For many people who are depressed, smoking becomes a means of self-medicating to treat their condition, temporarily improving their mood by increasing their dopamine levels. Unfortunately, the depressed smokers may get some relief from their suffering, but they are putting their lives at risk by doing so. Smoking is a deadly habit that can cause a wide variety of diseases ranging from cancer to heart disease.

For some, it may appear to be coincidence that people who are depressed often smoke cigarettes. The statistics, however, indicate that there might be more of a connection. Studies have shown that approximately half the people diagnosed with depression smoke cigarettes. Among the general population, the proportion of people who smoke is much smaller. According to a 2007 study by the Centers for Disease Control and Prevention, in the United States approximately 20.8 percent of adults (23.9 percent of men and 18 percent of women) smoke.

The exact nature of the link between depression and nicotine addiction remains a subject of great debate. Some researchers and doctors believe nicotine sometimes reduces the symptoms of depres-

Depression Self-Test

If you answer yes to even some of these questions, discuss your feelings with your parents and your doctor.

- Have you lost interest in hobbies and other activities that used to excite you?
- Do you feel tired most of the time?
- Have your sleeping patterns changed, making it harder for you to sleep or to get out of bed?
- Are you overwhelmed by sadness?
- Do you feel confused and like you cannot stop the pain in your life?
- Are you finding it difficult to go to school and complete assignments or to fulfill your obligations at work?
- Do you feel empty inside?
- Have your eating patterns changed so that you are eating less or more than usual?
- Are you plagued by anxiety or nervousness?
- Do you often feel irritable or restless?
- Are you pessimistic about the future? Does it look gloomy and difficult to you?
- Would you categorize yourself as pessimistic?
- Are you experiencing digestive problems, headaches, or other physical problems?
- Do you feel lonely and unloved?
- Are "worthless" and "guilt ridden" terms you would use to describe your feelings?
- Do you feel like things are out of control and that you are helpless to change your situation?
- Does the thought that "life is so difficult it is not worth living" ever cross your mind?

sion and improves people's moods. Other researchers are largely uncertain about the effects nicotine has on depressed people. Most can agree, however, that there is a complicated relationship between nicotine and brain chemistry.

CHAPTER 2

Glossary

affinity: an attractive force between people or things who share similarities.

connotations: ideas or emotions suggested by a word or thing.

desensitized: made less responsive to something.

efficacy: the ability to produce the desired result.

elation: a feeling of joy, pride, and hope.

euphoria: a feeling of great happiness and well-being.

insidious: slowly and subtly harmful or destructive.

Chemistry of the Depressed Smoker

For many years, there was a cultural stigma, or negative association, surrounding depression. People who had the disease were largely believed to be weak. Through willpower alone, they were supposed to be able to overcome this debilitating mental illness, which was thought to be simply an inability to cope with life's hardships. Asking for help with treating depression was extremely difficult because it meant acknowledging weakness and being exposed to the negative attitudes of others about the disease.

Today, depression is better understood by mental health professionals, doctors, and the public at large. While some of the disease's stigma remains, researchers have uncovered some

The effects of smoking on a person's brain chemistry can strongly influence their mood.

of its causes. Many factors cause depression, including external factors such as stress and loss and internal factors such as the chemical makeup of a person's brain. In fact, brain chemistry plays such a great role in depression that such antidepressant medications as Prozac® (fluoxetine) and Wellbutrin® (bupropion) alone often can help people overcome their depression.

How Neurotransmitters Work

Some people refer to the chemical cause of depression as a "chemical imbalance" because of the role played by chemicals in the body known as neurotransmitters. Scientists believe neurotransmitters have a major effect on a person's mental health. Neurotransmitters are chemicals that carry messages throughout the body, particularly in the brain. They work by binding to receptors on target cells in the brain and throughout the body. A receptor is a spot on a cell that acts very much like a lock. Each type of receptor can bind with the specific substance shaped to activate it but with no other, in the same way that a key can only open the lock it is designed to open. Each type of neurotransmitter acts as a key that activates specific types of receptors. For example, the neurotransmitter dopamine activates dopamine receptors, while the neurotransmitter serotonin activates serotonin receptors. When a neurotransmitter fits into its specific receptor, the receptor causes the cell on which it sits to perform some sort of action.

In the case of stimulating or excitatory neurotransmitters, when enough neurotransmitters activate enough receptors, an individual can develop feelings of *elation* and empowerment and have more energy. When too little of these neurotransmitters are available, however, fewer receptors are activated. This deficit allows the inhibitory neurotransmitters (the "stop" messages) to dominate, causing the activity in key parts of the brain to slow. Instead of feelings of happiness and energy, the person may feel sad, tired, and defeated. This is the basis for the chemical imbalance theory of depression.

Antidepressants

Researchers have developed medications to address some of the chemical imbalances that may contribute to depression. Antidepressant medications work on neurotransmitters in a variety of ways to help bring them back into balance. In general, they do this by increasing the amount of certain neurotransmitters available to the brain. They stop cells from reabsorbing neurotransmitters after the neurotransmitters have been used. These drugs help to recycle neurotransmitters, allowing them to be used again immediately rather than put into storage by other cells. This helps to keep them ready and available for use by the brain. It gives the brain more "go" signs, allowing it to return to a state of normal functioning.

Antidepressant medications are currently the first choice of most doctors and psychiatrists for treating depression. This is largely due to their *efficacy* and the ease with which they can be administered. Antidepressants alone can be successful in treating depression. Studies vary on the success rate, ranging from 50 to 65 percent of the time. When combined with another form of treatment, such as counseling or psychotherapy, their success rate climbs even higher.

Of course, medications are not the only drugs that can have an effect on a person's mood. In fact, people have

A doctor will often prescribe any one of several antidepressants on the market in an attempt to treat depression.

been using a variety of substances to treat depression for centuries. These substances have often done more harm than good, however. Tobacco is a prime example of this. Nicotine—the addictive chemical component in tobacco—also helps to bring more of the "go" messages to the brain.

The Chemistry of Nicotine

Many scientists contend that nicotine is one of the most addictive substances because it provides users with a pleasurable sensation. With its effect on mood, however, nicotine is also seen as a possible treatment option for those with depression.

Nicotine molecules fit perfectly into certain chemical receptors present throughout the body—particularly in

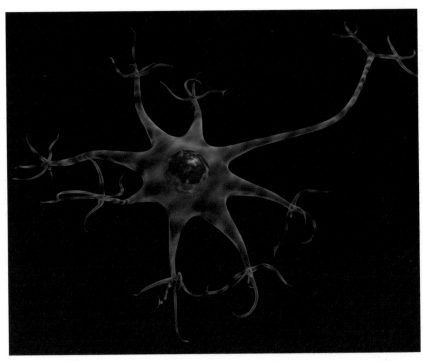

Nicotine interferes with the body's neurotransmitters and keeps neurons, like this one, from communicating like they should.

the brain—although nicotine is not produced or found naturally in the body. Because of their *affinity* for nicotine molecules, these receptors are known as nicotinic receptors.

Nicotinic receptors normally bind with a chemical called acetylcholine, an important neurotransmitter the body produces naturally. However, nicotine molecules actually have a much stronger effect on these receptors than does acetylcholine. When nicotine binds to a nicotinic receptor—when the nicotine molecules fit into the receptor like a key fits into a lock—it causes the receptor's cell to release great amounts of dopamine into the brain. Dopamine is a powerful excitatory neurotransmitter ("go" message).

When dopamine is released into the brain in this way, it causes what some people refer to as the "kick" or "high" of nicotine. This is often described as a sensation of mild *euphoria* or pleasure. The rush of dopamine stimulates certain parts of the brain, particularly those that control mood. Stimulating those parts of the brain produce pleasurable sensations. Many smokers say that after smoking a cigarette, they feel more alert and better able to concentrate. In some ways, this improved mood is similar to the feelings people report after drinking coffee. Indeed, some smokers use cigarettes as a quick "pick-me-up" in the same way many people use coffee.

Nicotine as an Antidepressant

Because of nicotine's mood-elevating properties, some doctors prescribe nicotine patches to

Some studies have suggested that nictotine can be used as a possible treatment for depression. However, there have been no conclusive results proven at this time.

nonsmokers as antidepressants. These patches deliver a small, consistent level of nicotine without most of the health dangers associated with smoking or chewing tobacco.

However, the use of nicotine as a treatment for depression is still relatively rare. Although a number of studies have shown that nicotine patches can be successful in improving the mood of depressed people, most health-care providers prefer to give their patients more typical antidepressant medications. Years of data concerning these medications' safety and efficacy are available, and they don't have the negative *connotations* that nicotine does. In addition, some insurance companies consider the use of nicotine as an antidepressant to be experimental and therefore are unwilling to pay for nicotine patches used to treat depression.

While no prescription is needed to buy cigarettes, taking up smoking is not a viable treatment for depression, even though many people with depression may use cigarettes to self-medicate. Smoking cigarettes causes more health problems than it could ever possibly solve.

The Problem with Nicotine

Part of the challenge of using nicotine to treat depression is that it is an extremely addictive substance. People who start using nicotine often find it very difficult—even impossible—to stop using it.

The same mechanisms that make nicotine pleasurable also make it addictive. When nicotine binds to nicotinic receptors, the dopamine rush it causes stimulates the brain, creating a pleasurable sensation. This pleasurable sensation is part of a chemical circuit known as the dopamine reward pathway. The dopamine reward pathway is a means for the brain to recognize and repeat actions it finds pleasurable. When the pathway is activated, the brain becomes flooded with dopamine, causing the sensation of pleasure. It is only natural that people would want to repeat behaviors that feel good. In the case of smokers, they want to smoke again to get that same nicotine "kick."

With repeated nicotine use, however, the brain gets used to increased levels of dopamine. Eventually, this causes the brain's chemistry to change. The nicotinic receptors in the brain and elsewhere in the body become *desensitized* to the nicotine that activates them. This means their reaction to nicotine becomes weaker and weaker, and they release less dopamine each time they are

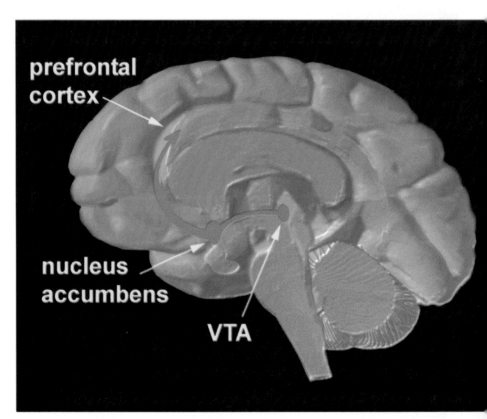

The dopamine reward pathway in the brain is stimulated by nicotine.

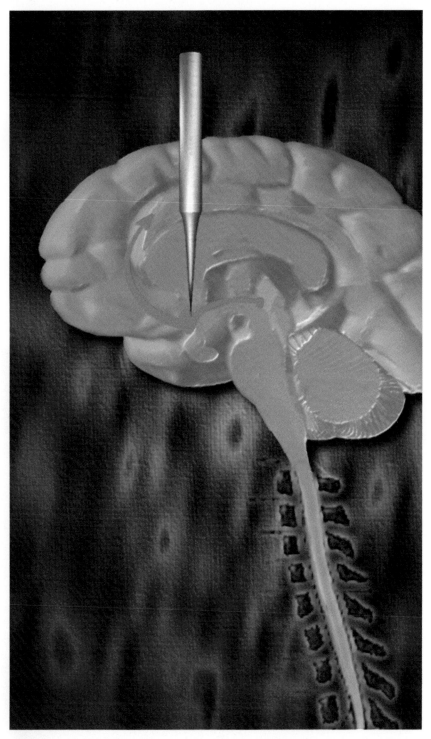

Stimulation of the dopamine pathway is associated with feelings of pleasure; over time smokers must increase their intake of nicotine to achieve this effect.

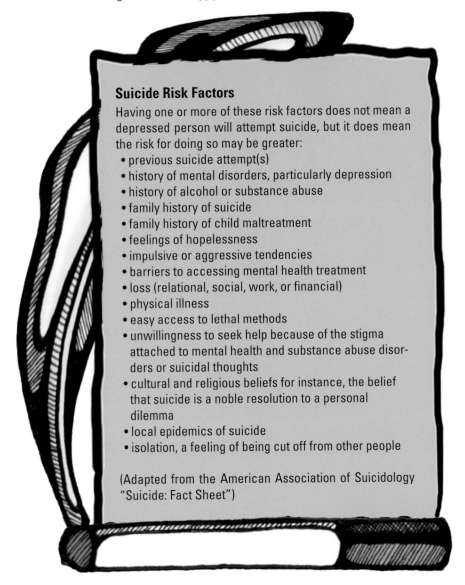

Suicide Risk Factors

Having one or more of these risk factors does not mean a depressed person will attempt suicide, but it does mean the risk for doing so may be greater:

- previous suicide attempt(s)
- history of mental disorders, particularly depression
- history of alcohol or substance abuse
- family history of suicide
- family history of child maltreatment
- feelings of hopelessness
- impulsive or aggressive tendencies
- barriers to accessing mental health treatment
- loss (relational, social, work, or financial)
- physical illness
- easy access to lethal methods
- unwillingness to seek help because of the stigma attached to mental health and substance abuse disorders or suicidal thoughts
- cultural and religious beliefs for instance, the belief that suicide is a noble resolution to a personal dilemma
- local epidemics of suicide
- isolation, a feeling of being cut off from other people

(Adapted from the American Association of Suicidology "Suicide: Fact Sheet")

activated. The name for this condition is tolerance. To achieve the same level of pleasure, the individual must take in a greater quantity of nicotine—in other words, smoke or chew more tobacco.

The brain also becomes accustomed to the increased amounts of dopamine it receives because of nicotine's effect on nicotinic receptors. If the dopamine level drops, the body begins to go through a process called withdrawal. The person can feel tired or sick, have headaches, and sometimes become grumpy or irritable. The body craves more nicotine while going through withdrawal. As a result, a smoker who is trying to quit will feel powerful urges to smoke a cigarette in order to increase the levels of dopamine in the brain.

Under such pressure, most people find they cannot help themselves. They smoke another cigarette. This, of course, reinforces the addiction, making it even more difficult to quit smoking. Not surprisingly, more than 80 percent of people trying to quit smoking have a relapse within a year, according to the National Institute on Drug Abuse.

The Health Costs of Tobacco

Nicotine addiction is only one of the dangers of tobacco use. By itself, nicotine is not a terribly dangerous drug. It can cause certain effects in the body, such as raising the heart rate, but these effects are generally temporary and not life-threatening. The other ingredients in cigarettes, however, pose a significant threat to a person's health and wellness. According to the American Lung Association, there are more than 4,800 chemicals in cigarette smoke.

The effects of using tobacco are *insidious*. Tobacco does not kill quickly, but rather kills a person slowly but inevitably. The damage tobacco does to a person's body is almost imperceptible at first, but builds up over the course of many years. Sometimes people are not even aware of the changes in their health caused by smoking until it is too late. But even when people do know the risks of smoking, the addictive power of nicotine will make it difficult for them to quit.

Smoking damages a person's health in many ways. It has been shown to cause a wide variety of cancers, including cancers of the lungs, stomach, bladder, and blood. The disease most often associated with smoking is lung cancer, which in the United States is the most deadly of all types of cancer in men and women. About nine out of ten cases of lung cancer are related to

One of the most common and well-known diseases caused by smoking is lung cancer; a diseased lung is shown here.

exposure to cigarette smoke. Overall, smokers are ten to twenty times more likely to get lung cancer than are nonsmokers.

In addition, smokers are as much as two to four times more likely to develop heart disease than are nonsmokers. Smokers are also more likely to experience strokes than are nonsmokers. These increased chances of illness are largely caused by tobacco's effects on blood vessels—the veins and arteries. The chemicals in tobacco can cause a person's blood vessels to clog with cholesterol and blood clots, dangerously reducing the amount of blood that gets through to important organs like the heart and brain. In the case of the heart, a lack of the oxygen, caused by the reduced or restricted blood flow, can trigger a heart attack. The brain also responds when it fails to receive oxygen, causing a stroke or "brain attack."

Tobacco smoke is associated with many other health problems. The lungs can become saturated with chemical residues from years of smoking. This can lead to difficulty breathing, coughing, and a serious medical condition known as emphysema. In emphysema, damage to the lungs causes them to become much less efficient, leading to extreme difficulty in breathing. A person with severe emphysema often has difficulty performing simple tasks, such as walking up a flight of stairs or putting away groceries, without having to stop to take a breath.

The Dollars and Cents of Tobacco and Depression

Both tobacco use and depression pose certain risks to individuals. They also have an impact on the world around them.

Depression is not only a potentially deadly illness; it is also an incredibly expensive illness because of its financial impact on the nation. Each year, depression costs American businesses more than $36 billion in lost productivity, which means thousands of days of work missed because of the illness. These types of statistics make it clear that treating depression should be a high priority for health professionals.

Smoking cigarettes, however, is not the solution. Cigarette smoking costs the United States about $193 billion each year. More than $97 billion of that total is from lost productivity and $96 billion of that sum is used to cover health-care expenses. The health costs of smoking also exact a heavy burden on society. Illnesses related to smoking—including cancer, heart attacks, strokes, and emphysema—claim about 438,000 American lives each year. Experts from the World Health Organization estimate that annually, more than 5.4 million deaths worldwide can be attributed to tobacco use.

With its lengthy list of associated health hazards, cigarettes are not the answer for treating depression. In addition, some researchers believe nicotine may actually *contribute* to depression.

Neurotransmitters and Other Mental Illnesses

Depression is not the only disorder that involves an imbalance of neurotransmitters. The cause of many mental illnesses and mood disorders can be traced back to various problems with the brain's neurotransmitters. Some experts believe that bipolar disorder, schizophrenia, and even certain phobias—irrational fears—are caused by problems with neurotransmitters. Not surprisingly, compared to the general population, a greater percentage of people with these disorders smoke cigarettes.

CHAPTER 3

Glossary

consensus: General or widespread agreement among the members of a group.

susceptibility: The likelihood of being affected by a specific thing.

Making Connections Between Nicotine and Depression

The percentage of depressed people who smoke is about twice that of the general population of smokers. This fact leads to interesting questions about the relationship between nicotine and depression. In many ways, scientists are in the early stages of understanding the links between the mental illness and the addictive substance.

Making Sense of a Mystery

As discussed previously, many people with depression use cigarettes to provide themselves with nicotine. According to some studies, the nicotine is used to treat some of the

Losing a job can help to trigger feelings of worthlessness or depression.

symptoms of depression. This thinking is partially based on the fact that nicotine causes a rush of dopamine to be released, which helps improve a person's mood. Numerous researchers' observations of smokers with depression and analyses of statistical data also support this assumption.

For example, one study showed that depression in people who are smokers is generally more severe than depression in people who have quit smoking or who have never smoked at all. There are two opposing but possible conclusions to draw from this study: people with more severe depression are more likely to be smokers than people with mild depression, or people who smoke are more likely to experience severe depression.

As they attempt to unravel the mystery of depression's link to smoking, researchers must examine all the possible conclusions they find in their work. As it turns out, the relationship is more complex than many people think.

Theories About Depression's Role in Smoking

Depression is a complicated condition. Unlike many other illnesses, such as the flu, depression does not have a single cause. The flu develops when an influenza virus invades the body. Depression, on the other hand, has a wide variety of causes, both internal and external.

Circumstances in a person's life, such as the loss of a loved one or a job, or poor performance in school, can trigger sadness and feelings of despair, frustration, and helplessness. Meanwhile, imbalances in neurotransmitters such as serotonin and dopamine can increase a person's *susceptibility* to feeling the crushing sadness of

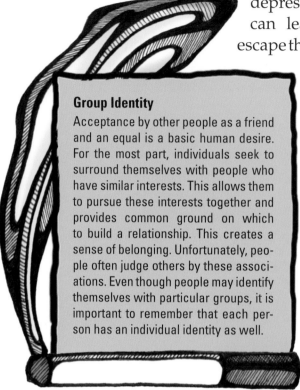

Group Identity

Acceptance by other people as a friend and an equal is a basic human desire. For the most part, individuals seek to surround themselves with people who have similar interests. This allows them to pursue these interests together and provides common ground on which to build a relationship. This creates a sense of belonging. Unfortunately, people often judge others by these associations. Even though people may identify themselves with particular groups, it is important to remember that each person has an individual identity as well.

depression. This imbalance can lead to an inability to escape that sadness even though circumstances may improve. Together, these factors can lead to depression.

Health-care professionals know some of the factors that can lead to depression, but pinpointing the actual causes in any one specific case can be extremely difficult. Like a jigsaw puzzle, researchers are piecing together the factors that lead to depression.

For this reason, saying people smoke in order to relieve the symptoms of depression is oversimplifying the relationship between these health concerns. It is true that some people use cigarettes to make themselves feel better when they are down, but that doesn't mean all depressed smokers use cigarettes for this reason. In fact, research indicates that a number of other factors may help explain the great number of depressed people who smoke.

Alienation

One reason some people with depression are more likely to smoke involves the social aspect of their illness. Depression is more than a biological disease; chemical imbalances in the brain cannot fully explain why people

Some young adults start smoking in an attempt to fit in with a certain social group or to make people like them.

Depression may lead to feelings of alienation; some people, especially young adults, may turn to cigarettes or tobacco in an attempt to fit in and find friends to get rid of these feelings.

get depressed. By the same token, the effects of depression are not merely biological. Depression affects a person's mood, ability to perform tasks well, and ability to relate to other people socially.

The social impact of depression can be particularly crippling. Many people with depression feel alienated from those around them. When a person feels alienated, he or she feels distant and isolated from others, as though he or she has nothing in common with those around him or her. People with depression are far less likely to make new friends and often lack the confidence and motivation to interact with other people socially.

Despite this, people suffering from depression—just like all people—have a need for belonging and friendship. For some of them, cigarettes might provide a means of bridging the distance they feel between themselves and others. To illustrate how this can work, consider a school. In most schools, there are groups of people who identify themselves and are identified by others by certain characteristics. For example, one group may be characterized as athletic, another as super-smart, and another as artistic. Some people may associate smoking with a certain group identity.

Someone with depression might begin smoking as a means of identifying with this group, thinking perhaps that he shares certain common experiences with group members. For this group, smoking has become a means of achieving a group identity. This, in turn, helps the depressed person feel closer to others in the group, thus decreasing the social isolation that depression may cause.

Just Can't Say No

Another theory about depression's role in smoking is that people affected by depression have a decreased ability to "just say no." Researchers already know that peer pressure is a major factor in making young people take up smoking. Very few adolescents who start smoking do so when they're alone. Usually, a person smokes his first cigarette with others, some of whom may also be smoking for the first time, while others may already be smokers.

Rationalizing Failure

Nicotine's grip is not necessarily an obvious one in the mind of the addicted individual. For the person contemplating quitting, his own mind may be his worst enemy. Many smokers rationalize reasons to continue smoking. That is, they think of logical reasons why they shouldn't quit smoking—at least reasons that are logical in their eyes. Ideas like "I can quit any time I want to; I just don't want to," or "Now just isn't the right time for me to quit," are common for smokers who are talking their way out of quitting.

Standing up to peer pressure can be difficult, particularly when the people involved are friends or role models. For those with depression, however, saying no in such situations becomes even more difficult. Depression affects more than just mood. It also impacts the part of the brain involved in reasoning and decision making. Just as depression has a negative effect on mood, it also has a negative impact on a person's ability to make sound, safe decisions. This is one reason people with depression are prone to self-destructive behaviors, including smoking.

For the person with depression, this impaired decision-making ability may take the form of decreased refusal skills. In other words, the depressed individual

If you are desperate to make friends, you may do things that go against your value system or that you would not do otherwise, like smoking tobacco.

may be less able to refuse an offer to smoke, even if that person would normally say no to such an offer. When in a situation in which others are smoking, someone who is depressed may simply go along with the crowd. He might make a different choice if he was mentally and emotionally healthy.

Self-Destructive Behavior

Another possible explanation for how depression leads people to smoke has to do with a characteristic of depressed people: they are more likely to engage in self-harming behavior. This is particularly true of adolescents with depression. These self-destructive behaviors can take a wide variety of forms.

Harm, in this sense, is not necessarily just physical injury or death. It can also involve a person's social connections, family, and future. For example, an adolescent who is depressed may be more likely to exhibit aggressive behavior at school. This behavior may lead to fighting, which would certainly be a way to inflict physical harm on oneself. However, it can also lead to the alienation of friends and others, detention at school, and punishment from parents. Usually, these are things young people want to avoid.

A young man who cuts his classes offers another example. This young man may seem rebellious to those around him. He may not seem to care what others, including his teachers, think about him. This may appear to be simply part of his personality, but in fact, it might be the way in which he reacts to his depression. Researchers have found that many young people experience depression differently than older people do. Rather than having depression that is characterized by sadness, many young people become moody, which can lead to more aggressive and antisocial behavior than is typical in older depressed people. The moodiness can make depression more difficult to diagnose in young people, because adolescence is a period of many changes. Moodiness is often as much a part of adolescence as physical and hormonal changes, so it may be dismissed as "normal."

Some young people with depression may start to smoke as a show of rebellion, a snub to authority figures

Depression can lead to self-destructive behavior. Sometimes these actions hurt mainly the depressed person himself, as in the case of smoking. But when other people are harmed by an individual's self-destructive behavior, there can be serious legal and social consequences.

and their rules. Ultimately, these adolescents may harm their standing in the eyes of people around them, distancing themselves from teachers, parents, and classmates. By taking up smoking, they are also exposing themselves to the physical damage caused by this habit.

Just Can't Quit

So far, all the ideas examined here to explore depression's effect on smoking have been theories. A theory is an unproven idea—an educated guess that provides a reasonable explanation of how something works. While theories can be useful for understanding and predicting possibilities, there are some facts available about the effect depression has on smoking.

For example, depressed smokers are much less likely to be able to quit smoking. There are many reasons why this is the case. Some have to do with the nature of depression itself, while others have to do with the nature of nicotine.

A person with depression often feels a crippling lack of motivation. This lack of motivation affects every aspect of that individual's life—from school and work to health and personal hygiene. The person with depression often finds it extremely difficult to do the things he or she knows he or she needs to do to make himself or herself a better person, including quitting smoking. Many people who try to quit smoking say things like, "This just isn't the right time for me to quit."

Another reason people find it difficult to quit smoking is the addictive power of nicotine. Trying to quit smoking at any time is terribly difficult. People often talk themselves out of quitting, finding plenty of reasons not to quit when they know they should. This is not merely a lack of willpower. Instead, it is evidence of the powerful grip nicotine has on people.

Depression leads to a lack of motivation,and it can be harder for a depressed person to quit smoking.

Nicotine's ability to help regulate and normalize mood makes it especially attractive and difficult to give up for many people who are depressed. For the person with depression, any improvement in mood that smoking may cause makes smoking seem especially valuable, even essential, to daily life.

Not everyone is convinced that nicotine has a positive impact on depression. Instead of being part of a solution, the chemical compound may be part of the prob-

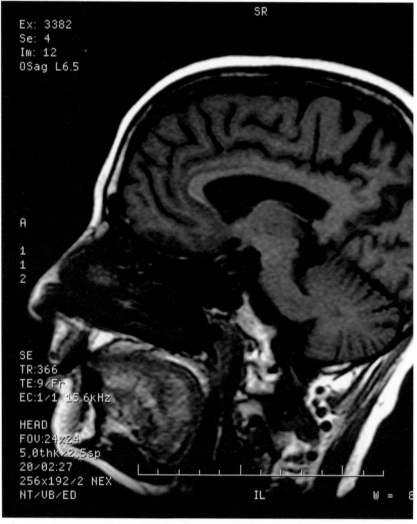

Some scientists suggest that nicotine use changes the chemistry of the brain itself over time; this could actually lead to depression.

lem. Some scientists believe that nicotine may actually play a role in causing depression.

Theories on Nicotine as a Cause of Depression

Research has shown that the relationship between nicotine and depression may not be a one-way street. In other words, not only can depression lead a person to smoke, but smoking may also be a factor in *causing* depression. A number of scientific studies examined nicotine's role in depression and found that in many cases, taking up smoking actually preceded the onset of depression. This is in stark contrast to the theory that depression leads to smoking.

It may be difficult to see how nicotine, which has antidepressant effects, can lead to depression. Blaming nicotine for a person's depression sounds a bit like claiming that taking aspirin will actually cause headaches rather than cure them. Even with its beneficial properties, nicotine may actually do more harm than good. Here are a few theories that shed light on how nicotine may lead to depression.

Changing Brain Chemistry

Long-term nicotine use can change a person's brain chemistry. Some scientists theorize that this is one way nicotine use might lead to an increased chance of developing depression.

When the brain is exposed to nicotine over a long time period—months or years—the nicotinic receptors become desensitized to nicotine. That is, they react less strongly to nicotine and therefore release less dopamine when they are exposed to it. This decrease in dopamine levels might lead to depression.

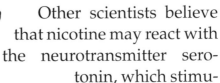

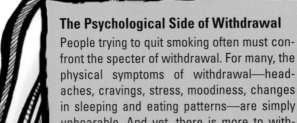

Other scientists believe that nicotine may react with the neurotransmitter serotonin, which stimulates the brain in much the same way dopamine does. These scientists think nicotine may interfere with the function of serotonin in the brain, causing it to become less effective in promoting a good mood.

These effects are not well understood. Nevertheless, they provide clues as to how nicotine may influence the development of depression.

The Psychological Side of Withdrawal

People trying to quit smoking often must confront the specter of withdrawal. For many, the physical symptoms of withdrawal—headaches, cravings, stress, moodiness, changes in sleeping and eating patterns—are simply unbearable. And yet, there is more to withdrawal than just the symptoms it produces. Many people discover that they relied on cigarettes for many things in their lives. Some people find they don't know what to do with their cigarette-free hands; others have a hard time socializing with others without smoking a cigarette. For some, being without cigarettes is almost like being naked. Together, the physical and psychological aspects of withdrawal undermine most smokers' attempts to quit.

Nicotine Withdrawal

Nicotine withdrawal is an unpleasant condition that occurs when people stop using nicotine after a long period of use. Many symptoms of nicotine withdrawal are similar to symptoms that are common in depression. People going through withdrawal may experience changes in their normal sleep patterns, bad moods, difficulty concentrating or thinking clearly, and changes in appetite and weight. Many people who suffer from depression report these same symptoms.

Nicotine withdrawal has many negative side effects, including aggression and
bad moods, changes in appetite, and difficulty concentrating.

These similarities have given scientists reason to believe that it may not be nicotine that causes depression. Instead, it may be nicotine withdrawal that leads to the development of depression. If this is the case, people who are trying to quit smoking might be at an increased risk of developing depression. They are then more likely to fail in their attempt; eventually, many people who try to quit smoking go back to their habit.

Unfortunately, there is no *consensus* among researchers on this point. Some studies have found that people who quit smoking are more likely to become depressed when they enter withdrawal. These same studies also found that people who are already depressed and quit smoking are more likely to experience worsening depression. Other studies, however, have found that quitting smoking has no effect on a person's mental state.

At present, no one knows for certain which theories are correct. While this may seem frustrating, keep in mind that research of this sort takes a great deal of time to conduct. Scientists, however, are optimistic that they will develop a clearer picture of just how nicotine withdrawal affects depression in the future.

So What Exactly Is the Relationship?

Scientists, doctors, and other health-care professionals are still trying to determine the exact relationship between nicotine and depression. Despite all the research conducted on the subject, there are still many unanswered questions. Research has answered a number of questions, resulting in a few certain facts.

First, there is a relationship between smoking and depression. It may seem strange to call this an important discovery when it is still unclear what the relationship is. For researchers, however, knowing that there is a definite relationship between the two is the basis for formulating the questions they will try to answer through their research.

Second, statistical analysis of the data from past research proves the relationship between nicotine and depression goes both ways. Depression increases the chances that people will smoke, just as nicotine increases the chances that people will become depressed. This information is important because it hints at some ways doctors can treat and prevent both depression and smoking. It also helps identify questions that still need to be answered.

CHAPTER 4

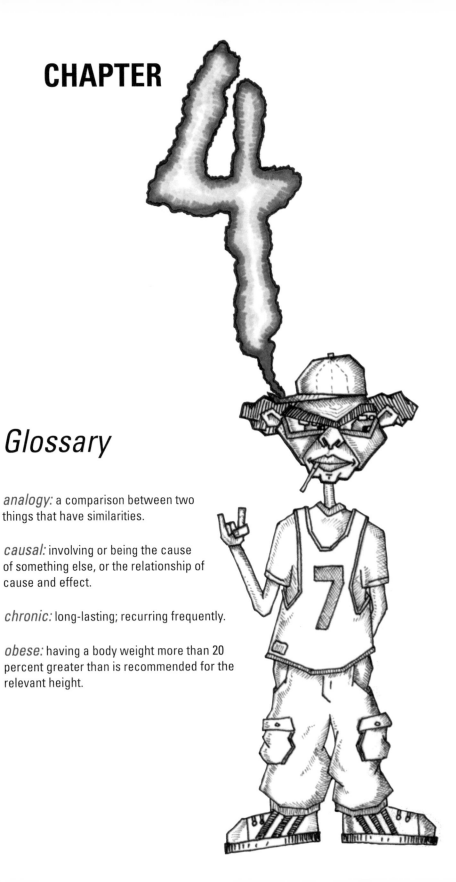

Glossary

analogy: a comparison between two things that have similarities.

causal: involving or being the cause of something else, or the relationship of cause and effect.

chronic: long-lasting; recurring frequently.

obese: having a body weight more than 20 percent greater than is recommended for the relevant height.

Many Unanswered Questions

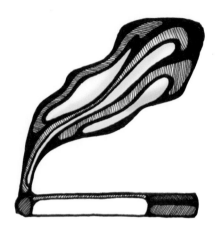

The theories mentioned earlier mostly pertain to the **causal** relationship between depression and nicotine addiction—how one thing can lead to the other. Two main causal relationships were discussed: depression increases the chance that a person will smoke, and having a smoking habit increases the likelihood that a person will become depressed.

Defining Noncausal Relationships

Not every relationship is causal, however. Consider the relationship between leaves on trees and the autumn season in the Midwest and the Northeast. As autumn approaches, leaves begin to change color and then fall from the trees. This may lead a person to believe that autumn causes the leaves to change. However, consider autumn in Southern California or Florida. The leaves in those places do not change color and do not fall from the trees, but it is still autumn. Therefore, the emergence of autumn and the falling of leaves are not necessarily related. It is actually something else entirely that causes the leaves to fall. In the Midwest and the Northeast, the number of daylight hours decreases as autumn gets under way. The shortened day means that the amount of sunlight the trees get also decreases. It is this decrease in sunlight exposure that causes the leaves to go through their annual fall passage.

Some studies suggest that the more time a student spends in school, the less likely they are to become either depressed or to start using tobacco.

While autumn and the changing leaves do not directly relate to the topic being examined here, the ***analogy*** can help illustrate the relationship between smoking and depression. In this example, the shortened days and decreased amount of sunlight cause the trees to lose their leaves. The change in sunlight is also a defining feature of the changing seasons. The changing of the leaves and the changing of the seasons, then, are linked by this common factor—the change in hours of daylight. Similarly, there are other elements involved in smoking and depression that can be studied to shed light on the subject. Some researchers and scientists have been trying to find the links they have in common. By finding the factors that are common to both, it may be possible to determine why depression and smoking often go hand in hand.

Noncausal Theories

Education

One interesting factor that influences both depression and smoking is education. People who are less educated are more likely to smoke. They are also more likely to suffer from depression. It is not a matter of IQ or grades but of the actual time spent in school and the level of education attained. People who finish college are less likely to smoke than are people who finish only high school. Similarly, people with higher levels of education are less likely to become depressed than people who have less education, according to some studies.

Young adults with low self-esteem may be more likely to become depressed or
to turn to smoking to escape their feelings of low self-worth.

There are a number of theories about why there is a connection between depression, smoking, and education. Some think it is because people with a higher level of education are more likely to find positive coping strategies when they experience stress. Coping strategies are ways of dealing with difficult times. People who have positive coping strategies are less likely to do things that are ultimately harmful, such as drinking alcohol, using drugs, or smoking cigarettes.

Others think this correlation has less to do with coping strategies and more to do with the things higher education affords people—better jobs and higher incomes. Statistically, the higher a person's level of education, the more money he or she will make. Most often, college graduates make more money than people who have finished only high school, for example. Studies also show that people who make more money are generally happier than those who just scrape by to pay their bills. Since cigarettes are used to help a person feel better and self-medicate for depression, a happier person may be less likely to turn to cigarettes than an unhappy person.

Self-Esteem

Low self-esteem is common in both depressed people and smokers. This is particularly true in young adults and teenagers, for whom issues of self-esteem are particularly important. This does not mean that all adolescent smokers and depressed people have low self-esteem but that a greater percentage of people who smoke or who are depressed report having problems with self-esteem.

Low self-esteem is common among individuals with depression. Many people who suffer from depression have feelings of worthlessness and powerlessness. They often feel as though they are not good enough. Self-

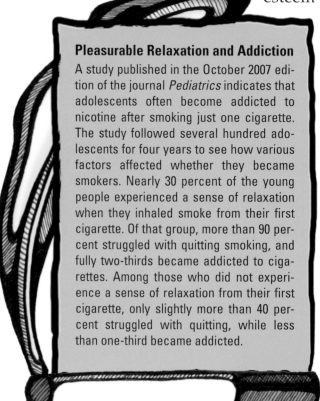

Pleasurable Relaxation and Addiction

A study published in the October 2007 edition of the journal *Pediatrics* indicates that adolescents often become addicted to nicotine after smoking just one cigarette. The study followed several hundred adolescents for four years to see how various factors affected whether they became smokers. Nearly 30 percent of the young people experienced a sense of relaxation when they inhaled smoke from their first cigarette. Of that group, more than 90 percent struggled with quitting smoking, and fully two-thirds became addicted to cigarettes. Among those who did not experience a sense of relaxation from their first cigarette, only slightly more than 40 percent struggled with quitting, while less than one-third became addicted.

esteem's link to depression is well understood. Its relationship to smoking is not as well defined.

A number of scientists have theorized that smoking may be a method of coping with low self-esteem and the frustration that often accompanies it. Many people who smoke say that cigarettes help give them a sense of "pleasurable relaxation." According to some surveys, this is the reason young people most frequently give for smoking. As discussed previously, smoking may also give a person a way to identify with an existing group or to become part of a new peer group. Particularly for people with low self-esteem, the feeling of belonging can be a strong motivator to smoke.

Body Image

Similar to self-esteem, body image is an important issue for people of all ages. It is, however, particularly challenging for young adults and teenagers. Body image refers to the way in which a person views his own body. Unfortunately, many people are dissatisfied with their bodies. This is referred to as having a negative or poor

Some people smoke in an attempt to lose weight. However, nicotine consumption is not a healthy alternative to dieting and exercise.

Many people. especially women, may suffer from low self-esteem because they see their bodies as ugly or lacking in some way.

body image. People with a negative body image may wish they were taller, thinner, more muscular, or more attractive.

Many people with a poor body image suffer from depression. People who are dissatisfied with their bodies and their appearances are more likely than others to feel unhappy, and this can act as a trigger for the development of depression. At the same time, however, it works the other way as well. Depression can *cause* a person to feel dissatisfied with her body. Women are significantly more likely than men, and younger people are more likely than older people, to have a poor body image. For most people with a poor body image, particularly women, feeling overweight is the main cause of dissatisfaction. And there is a clear link between smoking and obesity.

Some people consider smoking a weight-loss tool. In fact, many people who smoke lose weight, and many people who quit smoking gain weight. For this reason, an increasing number of people are using cigarettes as a weight-loss aid. Although male smokers outnumber female smokers, women are more commonly start smoking to lose weight than men do.

Being overweight or *obese* has its own set of health risks. Obese individuals are more likely to develop numerous *chronic* illnesses, including diabetes and heart disease. However, smoking is not a healthy alternative to more traditional weight-loss strategies, such as dieting and exercising. The benefits of weight loss brought about through smoking are never enough to offset the health problems tobacco causes.

Putting Knowledge to Work

At this point, the link between depression and smoking is, at best, poorly understood. Scientists studying the connection have determined that it is a complicated relationship. Given the complexity of both depression and nicotine's effects on the body, this is hardly a surprise.

Scientists know some aspects of the connection are causal. Smoking leads to depression, and depression makes people more likely to smoke. Other scientists have discovered that there are also some aspects of the relationship that are not causal. These researchers suggest that smoking and depression share certain common factors—characteristics common to both smokers and depressed people—that help explain why there is such

While no one is sure why this is the case, the connection between smoking and depression has been shown.

great overlap between these two groups. These common factors provide linkages between smoking and depression.

The best way to use this information is to allow it to help depression and nicotine addiction from developing in the first place. Hopefully, if the connection between these two can be severed, it will be possible to find ways to prevent them both.

CHAPTER 5

Glossary

cessation: The discontinuation of something.

complacent: Self-satisfied and unaware of possible dangers.

constraints: Things that limit freedom.

generic name: The non-brand name of a product.

trade names: Name given by a manufacturer to products or services.

Breaking the Chain

When it comes to the linkage between depression and smoking, knowing that there *is* a link is half the battle. The other half of the battle is applying that knowledge to help fight both depression and nicotine addiction. Unfortunately, much more information is needed. Researchers are continuing to collect more information to better understand the factors that link depression with nicotine addiction. Members of the scientific and medical communities have focused their attention on the issue and have uncovered a great deal of useful data, but more work remains to be done. In the years to come, new information will surface regarding the relationship between smoking and depression.

Many people refuse to seek treatment for their depression because they are ashamed and feel like people will look down on them for having a problem.

In the meantime, when it comes to the dangers of smoking, there is no reason to be *complacent*. Many promising theories point at possible avenues for treatment that may help to reduce both depression and nicotine dependence. With this information, health-care professionals and public-health advocates can begin to combat depression and smoking in new and exciting ways.

Treating Depression to Help People Quit Smoking

Stigma and Misunderstanding

One of the greatest problems in treating depression is recognizing the illness. An estimated two-thirds of people suffering from depression never seek help in dealing with their condition, according to the Depression and Bipolar Support Alliance. Most of these people suffer in silence.

Anyone who watches television has probably seen commercials advertising the multitude of medications available to treat depression. Although the condition can be treated, many people do not seek help. One of the major concerns of people with depression is the way others will view them if they admit they are depressed. Even after all the advances in understanding the causes of depression, the disorder still carries a powerful stigma for many people. They feel ashamed about being depressed, and this makes them reluctant to seek help for their condition.

For many people battling depression, a visit to a doctor's office may seem like an exercise in futility. Remember that depression is more than just a sad mood. True depression zaps away a person's motivation, self-esteem, confidence, and energy. A depressed person may not seek medical help because he or she does not believe anyone can help him or her. The person also may have such negative thoughts that he or she imagines that he or she will remain in an unhappy state forever and that there is no point in seeking treatment.

Stigma and Encouragement

While many people still attach stigma to depression and to the antidepressants that can treat it, smoking cessation has become a process that elicits admiration and the kind words of well-wishers and friends. This is because smoking itself has become highly stigmatized in today's society. The difference in public opinion about the two conditions is quite interesting, particularly when you consider that bupropion can treat both depression and nicotine addiction. Perhaps when more people feel it is okay to admit they are depressed, they will receive the same encouragement to treat it as smokers do.

Many people who are depressed do not realize how serious depression can be. They may not completely understand what is happening to them. They might think they should be able to get over their bad mood if it was brought on by stress or hard times. They may believe they will get over it if they give it more time. Unfortunately, that is not always the case. People often need medical or psychological help to overcome depression.

To ensure that individuals have the tools they need to understand their condition, information needs to be readily available. Health-care providers, teachers, parents, and even friends can play an essential role in making this information accessible. For those who are afraid to talk to someone, there are a number of print and online sources in which they can get more information on depression, its symptoms, and its treatment. This information can help people understand that depression is a true medical condition, not a character flaw or a weakness of will. When individuals understand this, perhaps they will no longer suffer silently when they are depressed, but instead seek the treatment necessary to end their depression.

Screenings

When people experiencing symptoms of depression do seek help, health-care professionals may not recognize the condition. In many cases, doctors miss the signs and

Depression is not caused by weakness or a character flaw. Instead, it is a diagnosable medical condition and should be treated as such.

symptoms of depression and fail to diagnose it properly. There are a number of reasons why doctors have such a hard time diagnosing depression.

Most health-care providers are under tremendous pressure to see many patients in a short amount of time. Given these time *constraints*, some doctors end up focusing on more visible health problems—things like a cough, fever, or pain. To make matters worse, depression can be a difficult thing to spot, particularly for a health-care provider who does not know the patient well. On top of that, many health-care providers are inadequately trained to spot and treat psychological illnesses, such as depression. Although they take coursework in these conditions, it is often only a small part of their education. Consequently, many doctors do not feel comfortable diagnosing or treating depression.

The solution in this case is fairly obvious, and it is one a number of professional organizations in the United States have already made a priority. These organizations have recommended that health-care providers receive better training in the identification and treatment of mental illnesses, including depression. They have also recommended that health-care providers screen many of their patients for depression, rather than just those who say they are depressed. The screening consists of a simple set of questions and observations that allow health-care providers to quickly, easily, and accurately determine whether their patients are depressed.

Once a doctor diagnoses depression, a treatment plan can be developed for the patient. After creating a plan, the doctor should

Better medical training can lead to more and better diagnoses and treatment of depression. If doctors know what is wrong, they can prescribe medication or therapy to help combat the problem.

continue to play an active role in the patient's care. Health-care providers must follow up with their patients to make sure they are taking their medicines and following their plan of care.

Antidepressants

For the majority of people with serious depression, antidepressant medications are the first choice of treatment options. The newest generations of antidepressants are considered safe, and they provide an effective means of battling this debilitating mental illness.

The stigma often attached to depression itself can also be linked to the medicines that treat the illness. In this case, many people feel that taking antidepressants is the same as giving up trying to deal with problems on their own. For these people, taking antidepressants is perceived as an admission of failure. The effective-

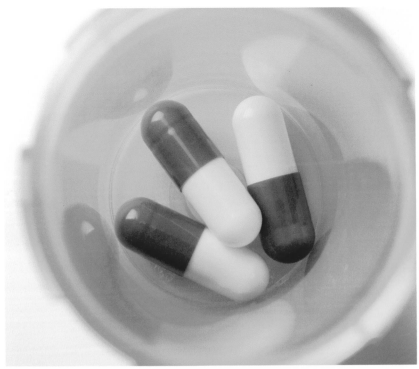

Antidepressants are often the first choice of treatment for people who suffer from depression.

ness of antidepressants in treating the chemical causes of depression, however, gives ample proof that depression is not merely a mood but a medical condition with physical causes.

By treating depression, health-care providers can also help to treat another problem—smoking. If depression has a role in causing people to smoke, then treating depression in smokers may help them to quit smoking more easily. With antidepressant treatment, depressed smokers will have a better chance of quitting, because they will have a more positive mind-set, greater confidence, and hopefully the motivation it takes to kick the habit.

This approach may help people who are depressed and trying to quit smoking. Many people with depression also smoke, so this pharmacological approach may have the ability to help many people who might otherwise not be able to quit.

Quitting Smoking to Treat Depression

A novel approach to treating depression may be to treat people's addiction to nicotine and to help them quit smoking. As studies have shown, smoking may have a role in causing depression. Helping people quit smoking while dealing with withdrawal symptoms that also contribute to depression may help combat this psychological disorder.

In recent years, a growing number of methods for treating nicotine addiction have surfaced. The most effective of these combine the use of medications designed to reduce one's dependence on nicotine with counseling or group therapy aimed at strengthening a person's resolve to quit. This combination of treatments is more successful than is any other treatment on its own.

People who want to quit smoking face a daunting challenge. The power that nicotine holds over the body, particularly the brain, is formidable. Many people find they cannot bear the withdrawal symptoms once they stop smoking. As a result, they fall back into their old habit and start smoking again. Various treatment options can reduce the likelihood of such a relapse.

Talk Therapy

One of the traditional methods of treating both nicotine addiction and depression is talk therapy. This refers to several different methods of treating addiction or men-tal-health problems that all focus on talking through

Group therapy is another option and is often used along with prescription medi-cations to treat depression.

problems and trying to change behaviors related to those problems. For example, in the case of smoking, talk therapy would focus on teaching the patient new behaviors and strategies to resist the temptation of smoking when a cigarette craving strikes. Talk therapy includes one-on-one counseling with a professional counselor, group therapy, and other similar treatment options.

In the days before antidepressants and other modern drugs were available, talk therapy was one of few options for treating mental-health conditions and addictions. Although today drugs are often the first choice of many health-care providers, talk therapy is still a useful and well-respected way to treat many conditions, including all sorts of addictions. There are also support groups, such as Alcoholics Anonymous and Nicotine Anonymous, that provide a form of talk therapy that can help people overcome addiction.

Although talk therapy has been used for decades to help people beat addiction, it has not been very successful in dealing with nicotine addiction. Because of nicotine's powerful grip on smokers, talk therapy is only successful in a small percentage of cases. At most, less than 20 percent of smokers attempting to quit will succeed if they rely on talk therapy alone.

If other methods of treatment are combined with talk therapy, however, it becomes much more effective. Today, a number of pharmaceutical treatment options exist that are fairly successful in helping smokers quit. These treatments are particularly effective when they are used in conjunction with some form of talk therapy.

Nicotine Replacement Therapy

Among pharmaceutical treatment options for smokers trying to quit, the most common one used today is nicotine replacement therapy (NRT). The nicotine individuals receive through NRT is delivered more safely than the nicotine they take in through smoking; those who use NRT are not exposed to the thousands of other chemicals released through smoking a cigarette. Through NRT, smokers avoid the withdrawal symptoms they would normally feel when they quit smoking, and those who do not experience withdrawal symptoms are more likely to stick to a smoking *cessation* plan.

NRT comes in a number of forms, including nicotine patches, nicotine gum, and nicotine sprays. The most common form is the nicotine patch, which is worn on the skin and delivers a constant dose of nicotine to the person wearing it. Nicotine patches are available in a range of dosage levels. These precise dosages allow people using NRT to slowly reduce the amount of nicotine they receive, eventually allowing them to stop needing nicotine altogether.

Not only does NRT provide a means of helping smokers quit smoking, it also acts as an effective antidepressant in some people. Not everyone responds to this treatment, but that is normal. Many medicines work well for some people but not for others. This is especially true of antidepressants and of nicotine when it is used as an antidepressant.

Given its ability to treat both nicotine addiction and depression, NRT is an obvious treatment choice for many smokers. By providing a constant dose of nicotine, NRT may help prevent depression in the quitting smoker who does not have depression, and it may also help the depressed smoker who is quitting keep from sinking

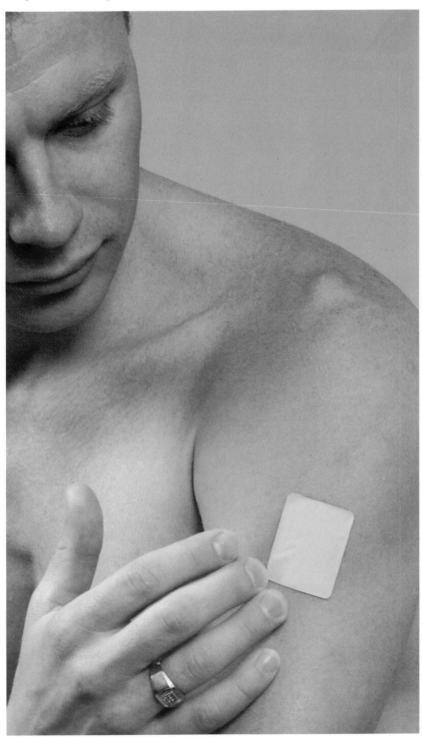

Nicotine Replacement Therapy, like this nicotine patch, can be used not only to help quit smoking, but as an antidepressant in some people.

further into depression. In both cases, NRT can do these things even as it helps the person quit smoking.

Antidepressants

Researchers have studied a number of antidepressants for their ability to help people quit smoking. For the most part, they are not very effective as smoking-cessation aids. One antidepressant, however, has achieved some positive results in treating both depression and nicotine addiction. That drug is bupropion, also known by its *trade names* Wellbutrin and Zyban.

Scientists and drug researchers are not certain exactly how bupropion works, particularly as an aid for people who are not depressed but are quitting smoking. They believe it has a number of effects on both nicotinic receptors and dopamine that help to decrease the cravings smokers have for cigarettes.

Research indicates that bupropion may be able to prevent nicotine from binding with nicotinic receptors. When less nicotine is able to bind with nicotinic receptors, less dopamine is released each time a person smokes. This causes smoking to become less pleasurable, which helps make nicotine less addictive. Ultimately, this may help the smoker quit smoking.

At the same time, bupropion increases the amount of dopamine that is constantly available to the brain. It does this by slowing the chemical breakdown of dopamine in the brain. By slowing this process, dopamine is available in the brain for a longer period. For smokers, this increase in dopamine may help to stave off cravings for cigarettes, which will help to prevent them from

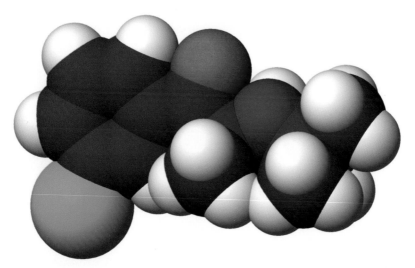

Chantix molecules are shaped similarly to nicotine molecules, meaning that they can fit into the nicotine receptors in the brain.

smoking. The increase in dopamine also works to combat depression.

Like NRT, bupropion offers the possibility of both treating depression and helping smokers quit smoking. By doing this, it may help ensure that smokers do not become depressed when they quit smoking, which in turn may help prevent them from restarting their old habit.

A New Drug in Use

The most recent addition to the arsenal of medicines available to help people quit smoking is called Chantix (*generic name* varenicline). Like bupropion, Chantix blocks nicotine from activating nicotinic receptors. This causes smoking to become less pleasurable and thereby helps decrease the addictive effects of nicotine. Chantix is so new to the market that very little research on its efficacy is available. However, it appears to be more effective than

Chantix helps alleviate withdrawal symptoms and allows people to live a normal
life while attempting to quit tobacco use.

bupropion in blocking the effects of nicotine. The U.S. Food and Drug Administration (FDA) approved the drug as a smoking cessation aid in 2006. Two years later, the FDA issued an advisory that indicated some users of the drug experienced "changes in behavior, agitation, depressed mood, suicidal ideation [thoughts], and actual suicidal behavior, according to an agency's press release. More research on the drug and its possible mental health side effects.

Risks of Taking Antidepressants
Although the new generations of antidepressants are safer and easier to use than older antidepressants, these medications do pose a major risk. People who take antidepressants may be more likely to commit suicide soon after they begin taking them. As an antidepressant medication starts to take effect, it raises people's energy levels before it improves their mood. Therefore, people who are still very depressed may find they have a great deal of energy, and they may channel that energy into self-destructive behaviors and actions. People just starting to take antidepressants must be monitored closely.

Like bupropion, Chantix also provides the brain with extra dopamine, which helps prevent the cigarette cravings and withdrawal symptoms that often lead a quitting smoker to light up again. While bupropion does this by slowing the action of chemicals that clear dopamine from the brain, Chantix does it by activating the nicotinic receptors.

The Chantix drug molecules are shaped a little like nicotine molecules, allowing them to fit into nicotinic receptors and activate them. The drug is not as effective as nicotine at activating the receptors, which results in smaller amounts of dopamine being released. Nevertheless, the amount of dopamine released is apparently

Never starting smoking is the best way to avoid discovering the links between nicotine and depression.

adequate to allow quitting smokers to avoid withdrawal. Initial studies show that Chantix is more effective than bupropion in helping people quit smoking. Like other treatments that help people quit smoking, Chantix may help prevent recurrences of smoking by staving off withdrawal symptoms.

All these methods are effective to some degree in helping the people who use them lead healthier lives. In the end, however, none of them is as effective as prevention. Never smoking at all is the best way to avoid discovering the links between nicotine and depression.

CHAPTER 6

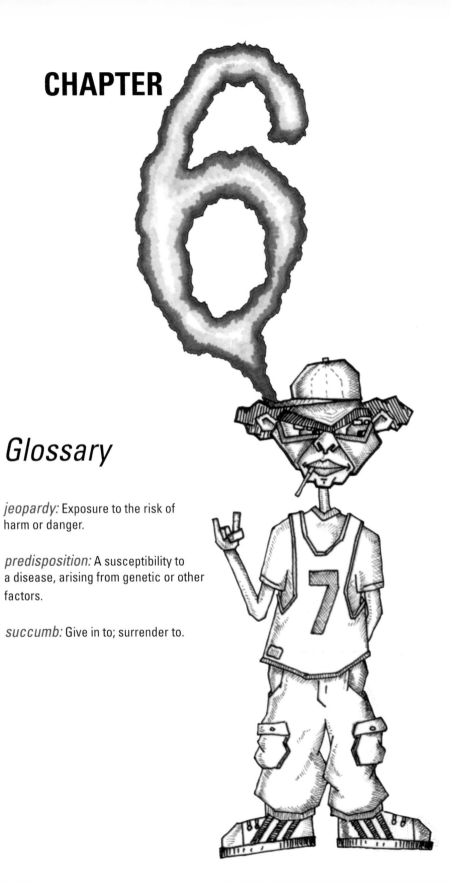

Glossary

jeopardy: Exposure to the risk of harm or danger.

predisposition: A susceptibility to a disease, arising from genetic or other factors.

succumb: Give in to; surrender to.

An Ounce of Prevention

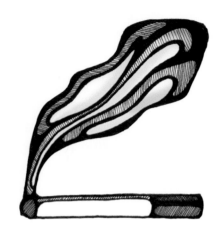

In most cases, there is no way to prevent depression from striking. After all, many circumstances in life are simply beyond any one person's control, such as the death of a loved one. Depression caused by a chemical imbalance can also strike unexpectedly. For individuals with a genetic *predisposition* to depression, its onset can be devastating. Unlike depression, however, addiction to nicotine begins with a preventable action—lighting up that first cigarette.

The best way to avoid becoming addicted to cigarettes and avoid becoming a lifelong smoker is to avoid smoking in the first place. A recent study provides evidence that many young people become addicted to nicotine after smoking just one cigarette—not one pack or one cigarette per day.

In addition, since it is known that depression leads to an increased chance of smoking and that smoking can cause depression, it makes sense that people should want to protect themselves against both conditions. Fortunately, many of the ways to do that are the same for each condition. These measures can help break the link between smoking and depression and help people lead healthier, happier lives.

Physical Activity

One of the easiest and most important things a person can do to maintain good overall physical and mental health is to exercise regularly. This does not necessarily need to be a trip to the gym to lift weights and run laps, though that is certainly a good routine for some people. People may find they prefer swimming; playing team sports, such as volleyball, soccer, or baseball; or even walking the dog every day. The key is to engage in pleasurable activity and to do it on a regular basis—at least three or four times a week.

Exercise is protective against both smoking and depression in a number of ways. For one, regular exercise boosts the performance of many important organ systems. Most notably, exercise strengthens the heart and improves b l o o d flow. This allows more blood—and with it more oxygen and

Exercising releases endorphins and sends more blood to the brain, both of which can make a person feel better mentally, decreasing the risk of depression.

Exercising can help with weight loss, which is a common reason why women
start smoking.

nutrients—to reach critical parts of the body, such as the brain. This added blood flow to the brain helps to improve mood, which assists in protecting the person against depression.

In addition, regular strenuous exercise can leave people with a sensation known as "runner's high." This is a pleasurable feeling that occurs during exercise that has been compared to the high a person might get from smoking cigarettes. The exact cause of runner's high is unknown. Some people think it is triggered by chemicals called endorphins that are released during exercise. Others say it is simply the feeling of accomplishment that accompanies a good game or workout. Regardless of its origin, the runner's high can provide people with a good feeling that may help replace the addictive high of cigarettes. It is also much safer.

Studies have shown that people who partake in less physical activity are more likely to smoke and more likely to suffer from depression than people who exercise regularly. Highlighting the link between depression and smoking, these studies also indicate a simple way to break that link—exercise. Exercise can also address another common concern—weight gain and body image. Particularly in women, weight concerns are a major reason for starting to smoke and for deciding not to quit. Weight concerns can also cause a negative body image, which may lead to depression. A good physical fitness routine can address these concerns and help a person feel better physically and emotionally.

This can help prevent depression and decrease the temptation to smoke.

Healthy Living

Physical activity is only one part of the puzzle, however. Exercise will improve a person's health, but it will be much more effective if combined with other measures, such as eating a healthy diet and practicing responsible living.

Nearly everyone knows the age-old expression "You are what you eat." In today's world, that statement can be ironic. Eating a lot of fast food, for example, will make a person anything but fast. And indulging in this type of food regularly may lead to one quick thing—weight gain. Fortunately, the habit of eating well is not difficult to develop. The key is to have healthy foods make up the majority of what is consumed, sticking to whole grains, fresh fruits and vegetables, lean proteins, and low-fat dairy products.

Healthy living will promote an overall feeling of well-being. This may influence a person's decision-making ability and mental health. For example, cars need to have the correct octane of fuel to run properly. If fuel with the wrong octane is used, the car will not run well and may

The Protective Power of Healthy Living

Healthy living protects people from becoming depressed and helps people avoid the temptation of smoking. This is not all it does, however. Living a healthy life by eating a balanced diet and exercising regularly can help prevent a great number of diseases, particularly those that develop later in life. While healthy living is not 100-percent guaranteed to ward off illness, it is certainly the easiest and cheapest way to promote good health throughout life.

Healthy living and eating can make a person feel better, making them less likely to make self-destructive decisions, like choosing to use tobacco.

even become damaged. The same is true of humans. Filling up with the wrong kinds of food may make a person have difficulties, too.

Coping Strategies

A final method for avoiding depression and smoking is practicing positive coping strategies. Coping strategies are the actions and behaviors that help a person deal with stressful situations, such as earning poor marks on an exam, going through a relationship breakup, or losing a family member or friend. Positive coping strategies are those that do not place people in any sort of *jeopardy*. They are safe and productive ways of dealing with stress.

Starting to smoke is a common method of coping with stress. It is not, however, a positive approach. Clearly, the health risks of smoking far outweigh any benefits that smoking may provide. There are many positive ways to deal with stress that are more effective than lighting up a cigarette.

Exercise, relaxation, meditation, prayer, talking to friends or family, painting, or going for a quiet walk in the park are examples of ways people have found to deal with their stress and negative emotions. The secret is to find something that alleviates some of the emotional strain. No matter the problem, it is important to take a break from the stressful situation in order to relax and find positive solutions to the issues at hand.

The benefits of developing positive coping strategies are practically boundless. Everyone faces stressful, frustrating, and sad times in life. The ability to deal with these times in a positive way will help people maintain mental health in the face of adversity. People who develop positive coping strategies will be much less likely to *succumb* to depression—and are also less likely to try smoking to help them relax or relieve stress. All in all, a person who practices positive coping strategies is more likely to lead a healthy and productive life.

Going to talk to someone, whether it be a psychiatrist or even just a trusted friend, can be an important choice for someone who is depressed.

Knowing Is Half the Battle

While there are apparent links between depression and smoking, more information is still needed. Clearly, scientists and researchers have yet to fully unravel the relationship between the two. A great deal more work needs to be done before anyone can say for certain exactly how smoking affects depression and how depression impacts smoking.

Nevertheless, a few things are known for sure. People who are depressed are more likely to smoke, and people who smoke are more likely to become depressed. The relationship between these two conditions is both causal and noncausal. The two conditions affect each other directly, and certain factors appear to make both depression and smoking more likely, including negative body image, weight concerns, low educational level, and low self-esteem.

Having this information is good. Using the information to make positive changes, however, is even better. Depression costs the economy billions of dollars each year. Smoking costs even more and claims hundreds of thousands of lives. It is important that people learn to live healthier, happier lives in order to avoid adding to these statistics.

What can people do to protect themselves? To start, they

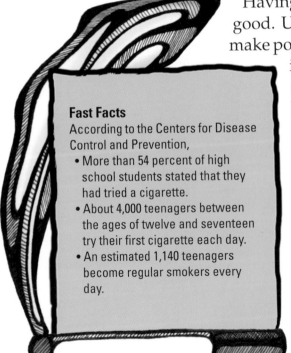

Fast Facts

According to the Centers for Disease Control and Prevention,

- More than 54 percent of high school students stated that they had tried a cigarette.
- About 4,000 teenagers between the ages of twelve and seventeen try their first cigarette each day.
- An estimated 1,140 teenagers become regular smokers every day.

The support of family and friends can help someone overcome both tobacco use and depression.

can do their best to lead a healthy life by getting plenty of exercise, eating a health-conscious diet, and spending time with friends and family. They can be aware of the symptoms of depression and seek help from a doctor or counselor if they feel they may be depressed. They should avoid smoking and encourage friends not to smoke through example.

In the end, it is the choices a person makes that determine whether he or she becomes a smoker. Peer pressure, life's hardships, and curiosity are all poor excuses for taking up smoking. The man who is being treated

While the choice to smoke or not to smoke is ultimately personal, there are many good reasons to say no.

for lung cancer or the woman in the psychiatric hospital who is waiting for her smoke break would probably say that the risks of smoking far outweigh any benefits it provides. When it comes down to it, the choice is personal.

Further Reading

Anderson, Judith. *Smoking*. North Mankato, MN: Smart Apple Media, 2005.

Balkin, Karen, and Helen Cothran (eds). *Tobacco and Smoking*. San Diego, CA: Greenhaven Press, 2004.

Connelly, Elizabeth Russell. *Nicotine = Busted!* Berkeley Heights, NJ: Enslow, 2006.

Copeland, Mary Ellen, and Stuart Copans. *Recovering from Depression: A Workbook for Teens*. Baltimore: Paul H. Brookes Publishing, Inc., 2002.

Esherick, Joan. *Clearing the Haze: A Teen's Guide to Smoking-Related Health Issues*. Philadelphia: Mason Crest Publishers, 2005.

Esherick, Joan. *Drug Therapy and Mood Disorders*. Philadelphia: Mason Crest Publishers, 2004.

Hyde, Margret O., and John F. Setaro. *Smoking 101: An Overview for Teens*. Minneapolis: Twenty-First Century Books, 2005.

Levert, Suzanne. *The Facts about Nicotine*. Tarrytown, NY: Benchmark Books, 2006.

McIntosh, Kenneth. *"Natural" Alternatives to Antidepressants: St. John's Wort, Kava Kava, and Others*. Philadelphia: Mason Crest, 2007.

Stewart, Gail B. *Understanding Issues—Smoking*. San Diego: KidHaven Press, 2002.

For More Information

Facts About Smoking
rex.nci.nih.gov/NCI_Pub_Interface/Smoking_Facts/
about.html

How Stuff Works: Nicotine
www.howstuffworks.com/nicotine.htm

Kids' Health: Smoking Stinks!
www.kidshealth.org/kid/watch/house/smoking.html

National Institute on Drug Abuse: NIDA for Teens: The
Science Behind Drug Abuse
teens.drugabuse.gov/facts/facts_nicotine1.asp

PBS: It's My Life: Smoking
pbskids.org/itsmylife/body/smoking

Surgeon General's Warning
www.gdcada.org/statistics/tobacco/surgeon/general.
htm

TeensHealth: Drugs & Alcohol
www.kidshealth.org/teen/drug_alcohol

TeensHealth: Your Mind
www.kidshealth.org/teen/your_mind

Time: Addiction and the Brain
www.time.com/time/2007/addiction

Bibliography

Centers for Disease Control and Prevention. "Economic Facts About U.S. Tobacco Use and Tobacco Production." <http://www.cdc.gov/tobacco/data_statistics/Factsheets/economic_facts.htm>

Croghan, Ivana T., Carrie Bronars, Christi A. Patten, Darrell R. Schroeder, Lisa M. Nirelli, Janet L. Thomson, Matthew M. Clark, Kristin S. Vickers, Randi Foraker, Kristi Lane, Daniel Houlihan, Kenneth Offord, and Richard D. Hurt. "Is Smoking Related to Body Image, Satisfaction, Stress, and Self-Esteem in Young Adults?" *American Journal of Health Behavior* 30 (2006): 322–333.

DiFranza, Joseph R., Judith A. Savageau, Kenneth Fletcher, Lori Pbert, Jennifer O'Loughlin, Ann D. McNeill, Judith K. Ockene, Karen Friedman, Jennifer Hazelton, Connie Wood, Gretchen Dussault, and Robert J. Wellman. "Susceptibility to Nicotine Dependence: The Development and Assessment of Nicotine Dependence in Youth 2 Study." *Pediatrics* 120 (2007): e974–e983.

Fergusson, D. M., R. D. Goodwin, and L. J. Horwood. "Major Depression and Cigarette Smoking: Results of a 21-Year Longitudinal Study." *Psychological Medicine* 33 (2003): 1357–1367.

Goodman, Elizabeth, and John Capitman. "Depressive Symptoms and Cigarette Smoking Among Teens." *Pediatrics* 106 (2000): 748–755.

Hitsman, Brian, Belinda Borrelli, Dennis E. McChargue, Bonnie Spring, and Raymond Niaura. "History of Depression and Smoking Cessation Outcome: A Meta-Analysis." *Journal of Consulting and Clinical Psychology* 71 (2003): 657–663.

Hunter, David. *Antidepressants and Advertising: Marketing Happiness.* Philadelphia: Mason Crest Publishers, 2007.

Lenz, Brenda K. "Tobacco, Depression, and Lifestyle Choices in the Pivotal Early College Years." *Journal of American College Health* 52 (2004): 213–219.

Lorant, Vincent, Christophe Croux, Scott Weich, Denise Deliege, Johan Mackenbach, and Marc Ansseau. "Depression and Socio-Economic Risk Factors: 7-Year Longitudinal Population Study." *The British Journal of Psychiatry* 190 (2007): 293–298.

Martini, Shahm, Fernando A. Wagner, and James C. Anthony. "The Association of Tobacco Smoking and Depression in Adolescence: Evidence from the United States." *Substance Use & Misuse* 37 (2002): 1853–1867.

Paperwalla, Khatija N., Tomer T. Levin, Joseph Weiner, and Stephen M. Saravay. "Smoking and Depression." *Medical Clinics of North America* 88 (2004): 1483–1494.

Picciotto, Marina R., Darlene H. Brunzell, and Barbara J. Caldarone. "Effect of Nicotine and Nicotinic Receptors on Anxiety and Depression." *NeuroReport* 13 (2002): 1097–1106.

Porth, Carol Mattson. *Pathophysiology: Concepts of Altered Health States.* Philadelphia: Lippincott Williams & Wilkins, 2005.

Prochaska, Judith J., Sharon M. Hall, Janice Y. Tsoh, Stuart Eisendrath, Joseph S. Rossi, Colleen A. Redding, Amy B. Rosen, Marc Meisner, Gary L. Humfleet, and Julie A. Gorecki. "Treating Tobacco Dependence in Clinically Depressed Smokers: Effects of Smoking Cessation on Mental Health Functioning." *American Journal of Public Health* 97 (2007): 12–15.

Smith, Deborah. "Smoking Increases Teen Depression." *Monitor on Psychology* 31 (2000). <http://www.apa.org/monitor/dec00/smoking.html>

Stuart, Gail. W., and Michele T. Laraia. *Principles and Practice of Psychiatric Nursing.* St. Louis: Elsevier Mosby, 2005.

Vogel, Julie S., David P. Hurford, Janet V. Smith, and AmyKay Cole. "The Relationship Between Depression and Smoking in Adolescents." *Adolescence* 38 (2003): 57–74.

Index

Picture Credits

Centers for Disease Control and Prevention (CDC)
 Dr. Ewing, Edwin, Jr. p. 36

Corbis: p. 83

Dreamstime
 Doctorkan: p. 12
 Goodynewshoes: p. 43
 markstout: p. 88
 photowitch: p. 102
 Sebcz: p. 86
 Zweig 17: p. 22

Eyewire: p. 47

istockphoto.com : pp. 51, 60, 65, 66, 97
 Adrian, Roberto: p. 68
 Ball, Jan, p.75
 Balderas, Christine p. 78

Bobbieo: p. 55
Casarsa, Valentin p. 15
Cox, Dennis: p. 99
Dra_schwartz: p. 25
Freitas, Kim: p. 81
Hime, Alisha p. 44
Harman, Tim 49
Iasek: p. 26
Thompson, Leah-Anne, pp. 28, 41
 Torres, Carlos Luis: p. 52

Jupiter Images: pp. 60, 66,72, 96

National Cancer Institute
 Bartlett, Linda: p. 16
National Institute on Drug Abuse (NIDA): pp. 30, 31

Office of Applied Statistics (OAS): pp. 16

To the best knowledge of the publisher, all other images are in the public domain. If any image has been inadvertently uncredited, please notify Harding House Publishing Service, Vestal, New York 13850, so that rectification can be made for future printings.

Author/Consultant Biographies

Author

David Hunter is the author of a number of books on health and wellness issues targeted toward young people. He served in the Peace Corps as a junior high–level teacher in the Central Pacific island country of Kiribati. He is currently studying nursing at Johns Hopkins University and is working as a clinical nurse extern at Johns Hopkins Hospital.

Consultant

Wade Berrettini, the consultant for *Smoking: The Dangerous Addiction*, received his MD from Jefferson Medical College and a PhD in Pharmacology from Thomas Jefferson University. For ten years, Dr. Berrettini served as a Fellow at the National Institutes of Health in Bethesda, Maryland, where he studied the genetics of behavioral disorders. Currently Dr. Berrettini is the Karl E. Rickels Professor of Psychiatry and Director, Center for Neurobiology and Behavior at the University of Pennsylvania in Philadelphia. He is also an attending physician at the Hospital of the University of Pennsylvania.

Dr. Berrettini is the author or co-author of more than 250 scientific articles as well as several books. He has conducted ground-breaking genetic research in nicotine addiction. He is the holder of two patents and the recipient of several awards, including recognition by Best Doctors in America 2003–2004, 2005–2006, and 2007–2008.